TONY
BENNETT
1926–2023
COLUMBIA
RECORDS
CBS
CRC 29
MW01625747

# LIFE
# TONY BENNETT

**Dotdash Meredith Premium Publishing**
EDITOR IN CHIEF Kostya Kennedy
CREATIVE DIRECTOR Gary Stewart
EDITORIAL OPERATIONS DIRECTOR Jamie Roth Major
MANAGER, EDITORIAL OPERATIONS Gina Scauzillo
EDITOR Steve Dougherty
MANAGING EDITOR Robert Sullivan (2014 edition)
ART DIRECTOR Li'l Robin Design, Inc. (2014 edition)
WRITER-REPORTERS Marilyn Fu, Amy Lennard Goehner, Daniel S. Levy (all 2014 edition)
COPY EDITORS Barbara Gogan, Joel Van Liew (both 2014 edition), Tracy Guth Spangler
SENIOR PHOTO EDITOR C. Tiffany Lee
PHOTO EDITORS Robert Conway, Steph Durante, Rachel Hatch, Louis Pearlman
ASSOCIATE PHOTO EDITORS Sarah Cates (2014 edition), Kwailan Chin
CONSULTING PICTURE EDITOR Tom Tierney (2014 edition)
DIRECTOR OF PHOTOGRAPHY Christina Lieberman (2014 edition)
REPORTER Ryan Hatch
PRODUCTION DESIGNER Sandra Jurevics
PREMEDIA TRAFFICKING SUPERVISOR Greg Fairholm
PREMEDIA IMAGING SPECIALIST Jacques Lizotte
COLOR QUALITY ANALYST John Santucci

VICE PRESIDENT & GENERAL MANAGER Jeremy Biloon
VICE PRESIDENT, GROUP EDITORIAL DIRECTOR Stephen Orr
SENIOR DIRECTOR, BRAND MARKETING Jean Kennedy
ASSOCIATE DIRECTOR, BRAND MARKETING Katherine Barnet
SENIOR MANAGER, BRAND MARKETING Geoffrey Wohlgamuth
BRAND MANAGER, BRAND MARKETING Mia Rinaldi

SPECIAL THANKS Gabby Amello, Brad Beatson

**Dotdash Meredith**
PRESIDENT, LIFESTYLE Alysia Borsa

PRINTED IN THE USA

**FRONT COVER** Simon Ritter/Redferns/Getty
**BACK COVER** Michael Ochs Archives/Getty
**TITLE PAGE** Herman Leonard
**THESE PAGES** Guy Gillette

INTRODUCTION

# A NATIONAL TREASURE

BY STEVE DOUGHERTY

The show biz ladder had few rungs lower than Anthony Dominick Benedetto's gig at Riccardo's, the Italian restaurant in his hometown, Astoria, Queens, New York, where, at 16, he worked as a singing waiter. But the artist the world came to know as Tony Bennett worked the dining room the same way he would the Copa or Carnegie Hall—he gave it his all. "We'd get a request from a customer and then I'd run back into the kitchen to work out the arrangements," he recalled in his 1998 memoir, *The Good Life*. "I really cut my teeth as a performer at that job." His dreams then did not extend beyond the beckoning lights of nearby Manhattan. "When you'd see this big city," he told the *New York Times* decades later, "you'd say, 'Boy, wouldn't it be great to become famous in that great city there?'" Tony Bennett and his music would conquer territories far beyond the island of Manhattan. "If America is a song," Anthony Hopkins said in the narration of a 2007 PBS *American Masters*, "Tony Bennett is its singer."

By the time of his death on July 21 at age 96, Bennett was more than a national treasure. "I Left My Heart in San Francisco," was his signature. But he put his heart into every song and the bel canto—the "beautiful music"—of his voice was heard around the world. "When it comes to heart," critic (and *Good Life* coauthor) Will Friedwald wrote, "Bennett is a virtuoso."

He leaves a legacy greater than his 50 million albums sold, his 90-plus singles, his 19 Grammy Awards amassed in a hit-making career that began in 1950 and found him still at it, releasing acclaimed albums, performing and even touring, well into his nineties. Long running acts of a younger generation like Bob Dylan and the Rolling Stones will have to remain on the road another full decade and more to match Bennett's longevity. Collaborations with music giants from Duke Ellington and Count Basie to 21st-century stars such as Amy Winehouse and Lady Gaga earned accolades in genres and music epochs that span the history of popular music from the post–World War II era to today.

KEVIN MAZUR/WIREIMAGE/GETTY

The son of Italian immigrants—his father, Giovanni, emigrated at age 11; his mother, Anna, crossed the ocean in utero and was born in America—Bennett came from a long line of singers on his father's side. "Singing," he wrote, "is in my blood." A mobbed-in-the-streets pop idol at 25, his star dimmed during the reigns of Elvis and the Beatles. But it was secured, thanks in part to "San Francisco," the 1962 smash that kept his music in the air throughout a decade that saw the careers of contemporaries go into near permanent eclipse. At the same time, Bennett, a passionate and lifelong civil rights advocate, earned an honored place in the annals of the movement when he marched alongside Martin Luther King in 1964.

Beset in the 1970s by drug and money problems, he engineered a startling career resurgence in the following decades. "Tony Bennett has not just bridged the generation gap," the *New York Times* wrote of his Grammy-winning 1994 *MTV Unplugged* performance, "he has demolished it."

Indeed, his dimpled grin, like his gleaming green eyes, Roman nose and nobly tailored tuxedos, became as familiar to new generations of fans as his exultant performances, his devotion to the Great American

MICHAEL OCHS ARCHIVES/GETTY

THE ALBUMS ARE already piling up in 1970 (left). His debut, *Because of You,* was released in 1952. There will be more than 90 albums in all, including compilations and collaborations, like 2014's *Cheek to Cheek* with Lady Gaga, making him, at age 88, not only the coolest, but also the oldest living artist to land at No. 1 on *Billboard*'s Top 200 album chart. As I wrote for the liner notes of his 2013 disc, *Live at the Sahara: Las Vegas, 1964*: "You will find no agreement as to when Tony Bennett was (or is or will be) at his best . . . He may be better tomorrow. He would wager that he will be. How wonderful is that? A man who made this music that we hear, and made it back in 1964 in the Congo Room at the Sahara, is still seeking, night after night, to be just as good—or even better. There has never been anything like Tony Bennett."

—Robert Sullivan

Opposite: Tony and Susan at the Metropolitan Museum of Art in New York.

Songbook classics and his unwavering optimism. "I've been singing for 60 years," Bennett exclaimed at the 2005 Monterey Jazz Festival. "If I get lucky enough I'd like to sing for another 60 years. Beautiful!"

Through most of his later decades, Bennett enjoyed the good life indeed. After two otherwise failed marriages—the first produced two sons, D'Andrea (Danny) and Daegel (Dae, for short); the second, daughters Joanna and Antonia—he wed his long-time companion Susan Crow, a former New York City social studies teacher turned artist manager, in 2007. He devoted himself to another lifelong passion, painting, and to his and his wife's arts education foundation. In a kind of monument to Bennett's modesty, the New York City public school for performing and visual arts that he and his wife founded in his native Astoria is named not for Bennett but for his own musical hero, Frank Sinatra. In February 2021, his wife and sons revealed that Bennett had Alzheimer's, the progressive, debilitating form of dementia that had first been diagnosed in 2016. While ravaging so much of life that he held dear, the disease had, almost miraculously it seemed, left his gift intact, allowing him to perform in concert right up until he gave his final public performance in August 2021. Thereafter he continued to perform at home, encouraged by his family and caregivers for singing's theraputic value. "There's a lot about him that I miss," Susan told AARP magazine in 2021. "Because he's not the old Tony anymore." After a pause to steady her voice, she added, "But when he sings, he's the old Tony."

Tony Bennett was 88 years old in 2014 when LIFE first published this collection of photos culled from the magazine's archives as well as many never-before-seen shots provided by the singer himself. This updated edition includes an expanded version of the original text written by LIFE's Robert Sullivan, who knew Bennett both as an interview subject and as a friend. This extraordinary collection of words and images delivers an intimacy that allows us to share an extraordinary life as it was being lived. As Bennett would say: "Beautiful!"

FOREWORD

# TONY MADE THE PICTURES CLEARER

BY MARTIN SCORSESE

*On the occasion of his 75th birthday party, a grand affair at the Metropolitan Museum of Art in New York City—various comments and tributes were offered. The ones by film director Martin Scorsese were particularly eloquent and, in leading into a book of photography, apt. He allowed them to be reprinted here as the foreword to our volume.*

PETER KRAMER/GETTY

**AUGUST 2, 2001**

In acting it's called "sense memory." That's what Tony Bennett's voice is for me.

When I hear his music, a certain time and place come alive for me again. Whenever I hear that wonderful voice, that voice that's as familiar and intimate and accessible as the voice of someone from your own family, it all comes back to me in a flash.

When I was growing up in Little Italy, music drifted in from everywhere. I watched everything that went on outside the windows of our apartment. The good, the bad and the mundane—it was all scored by music coming from radios in passing cars, from storefronts or out of other apartment windows. It was as if my life itself was scored by these songs. I suppose that's why music has always been so important to me as a filmmaker. Because in fact, it was that music which inspired me to interpret the world around me.

When I hear "Rags to Riches," I really *see* that world gone by. I *feel* it, the neighborhood where I grew up, in all its particulars—the texture of the paint on the walls, the clothes people wore (and the way they wore them), the way people moved, spoke, behaved. I hear the song, and I relive the essence of a specific time and place, in a particular community and in American culture.

I was eight or nine when "Rags to Riches" became a hit. It had this instantly commanding sound—the brass, the haunting reverb effect, and, of course, the soulful, wonderfully authoritative voice that cut right through it all.

When I started making films, I often found that once I heard the music, I could see the picture. In many ways, this started for me with Tony Bennett's music. His songs made the picture clearer for me—they helped me to visualize when and how the camera should move, where an actor should be in the frame, what the light should be like. Creating the worlds of *Mean Streets, Raging Bull* and *GoodFellas* would have been unthinkable without Tony Bennett.

KEVIN MAZUR/WIREIMAGE/GETTY

**THIS IS WILD: TONY SWINGING** a couple of tunes in front of this huge Egyptian sandstone ruin from 15 B.C. It's his 75th birthday party and it's being held in the Temple of Dendur gallery at the Metropolitan Museum of Art, above, in 2001. Martin Scorsese, left, with Tony in 2004, pays tribute along with scores of friends and well-wishers.

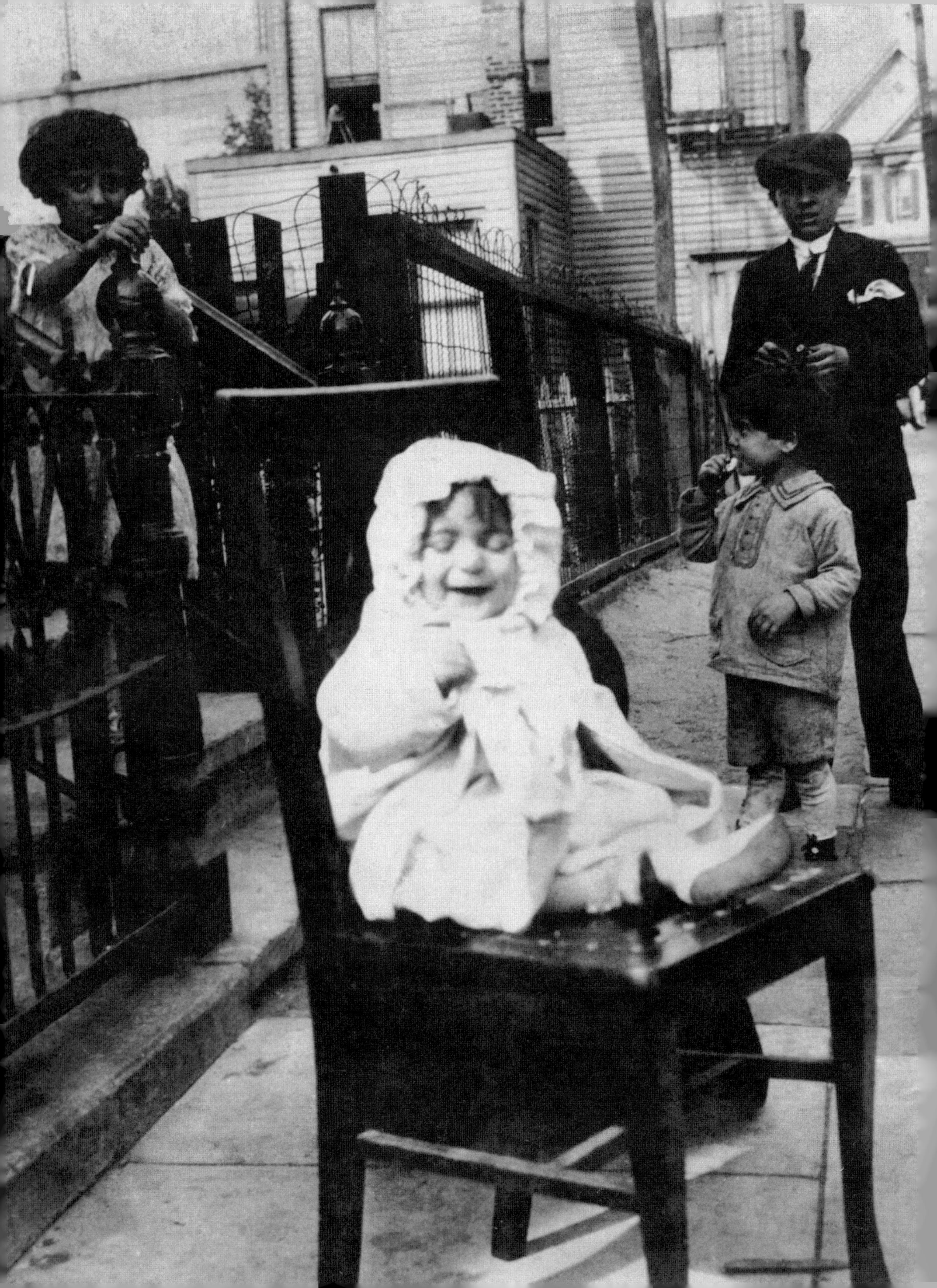

# A KID FROM QUEENS 1926–1943

**HIS STARS ARE ALIGNING** even before he is born, at St. John's Hospital in Long Island City, Queens, New York, on August 3, 1926. Anthony Dominick Benedetto's Calabria, Italy–born father, Giovanni, "had a wonderful singing voice," Tony Bennett recalls in his 1998 memoir, *The Good Life,* written with Will Friedwald. "He would often climb to the top of the mountains in Calabria and sing out to the whole valley below. Singing is a part of my heritage. I'm convinced it's in my blood, and that's why I'm a singer today." After Giovanni emigrated to America in 1906 at age 11, and in 1919 married his first cousin Anna (née Suraci), the couple lived in an apartment above a grocery store in midtown Manhattan, where Giovanni (by then, John) worked for his uncle. The building, at the corner of Sixth Avenue and 52nd Street, stood on the future site of Columbia Records' famous "Black Rock" headquarters. "I was told by one of the presidents of the company that sales of my records subsidized at least 10 floors of that building!" writes Tony, the grocery clerk's son destined to be one of the label's top stars. Sadly, his father was already suffering heart problems by the time Tony was born and, within a year, he was unable to work. As a result, Tony tells me decades later, speaking in that pensive, soft way of his: "I grew up in poverty." A pause, just there. "Another thing that makes where I landed so unbelievable," he adds. Opposite: Already, that smile.

COURTESY OF THE BENEDETTO FAMILY

COURTESY OF THE BENEDETTO FAMILY

**"A VERY POETIC, SENSITIVE** man," Tony says of his father, "full of love and warmth." In the photograph at right, young Tony is seated next to papa John among a gathering of the tightly knit family in Pyrites, New York. It is devastating for the boy, 10 years old, when his father dies of congestive heart failure at age 41. Shortly after, Tony is sent to live for a time with an aunt and uncle in distant Pyrites, near the Canadian border. "I couldn't believe that this wonderful, beautiful man was really out of my life and that I would never see him again," Tony writes in *The Good Life*. "I was heartbroken. My eyes welled up with tears and I wept."

BOTH OF TONY'S OLDER siblings, Mary and John (with their little brother in the photo at left), were born in their parents' Manhattan apartment, on the site of the future Black Rock. Tony, the first in his family born in a hospital, grows up in Astoria, Queens, in a household besotted with music. His opera-loving brother John (below with Tony and their parents and grandmother) is a sensational singer of arias. He performs solos at the Metropolitan Opera as a young teen and is dubbed "Little Caruso" by the New York press. Their uncle Dick is a hoofer in vaudeville and Tony enjoys entertaining the family with popular Eddie Cantor and Al Jolson tunes of the day. Tony's own star first shines at age 10 in 1936 when he sings "Marching Along Together" at Mayor Fiorello La Guardia's side as they parade across the brand-new Triborough Bridge during gala opening ceremonies. Opposite: Tony recalls it cost a nickel for him and his sibs to pose with a neighborhood steed.

COURTESY OF THE BENEDETTO FAMILY (3)

COURTESY OF THE BENEDETTO FAMILY (2)

"I HAD A BEAUTIFUL FAMILY," Tony recalls during a conversation at his apartment in Manhattan, smiling warmly at the memory of lively weekend gatherings of his many relatives. "We'd make a circle, and the entertainment was my brother, my sister and myself. We'd stand inside the circle, and they're all sitting around us with guitars and mandolins, and they'd have us perform for them." At age 16 Tony left school to help support his family, working as a newspaper copy boy and later as a singing waiter. Opposite are Mary, Tony, John with their father. At right are John and Tony with Grandpa Suraci.

COURTESY OF THE BENEDETTO FAMILY

# YOU'RE IN THE ARMY NOW 1944–1946

**"ONE MINUTE IT WAS A PEACEFUL** Sunday afternoon, and the next we were at war." Tony Bennett is a 15-year-old high schooler with soaring ambitions on December 7, 1941. He and his family are returning from a traditional Sunday gathering—a song or two from Tony no doubt on the menu—when they hear newsboys shouting in the streets: "Extra! Extra!" A place he's never heard of, Pearl Harbor, has been attacked, and life will never be the same. Tony turns 18 in 1944 and is drafted into the Army and sent overseas, his dreams of a music career deferred. He suffers the terrors of combat in France and Germany, where the incomprehensible awaits: He witnesses first hand the horrors of the holocaust when his infantry unit liberates a concentration camp near Landsberg. When his homecoming is delayed after war's end, he finds himself, as in the photo at left, entertaining troops and civilians, a kind of basic training for what will become his life's work.

COURTESY OF THE BENEDETTO FAMILY

TONY IS A PATRIOT AND HE'S proud, but he would emphasize always that he has long been a pacifist. "The main thing I got out of my military experience was the realization that I am completely opposed to war," he writes in his memoir. "Every war is insane, no matter where it is or what it's about. Fighting is the lowest form of human behavior. It's amazing to me that with all the great teachers of literature and art, and all the contributions that have been made on this very precious planet, we still haven't evolved a more humane approach to the way we work out our conflicts." At left, Tony is flanked by his best Army buddy and fellow New Yorker Freddy Katz, left, and his brother Stan. Freddy plays piano in some of the same regimental bands Tony sings with once the shooting ends. Back in the states Tony stays in touch with the brothers and becomes close with their entire family, a lively and cultured group of musicians, artists and intellectuals. Freddy and Stan's brother, Abe, first trumpet in the Metropolitan Opera Orchestra, helps Tony learn something about his own instrument, teaching him, Tony writes, "how to breathe correctly when I was singing."

**A SWING BAND OF BROTHERS:** After Germany surrenders, Tony stays on in Europe as part of the occupying force. In the photos opposite, he enjoys the peace with fellow members of the 255th Regiment band he performs with in Germany. But searing memories of war are not fast fading. "I watched as my buddies died right before my eyes," Tony writes in his memoir. "All I could think of was 'When am I gonna get it?'" He recalled General George Patton waking the recruits on the eve of their first battle. "'Now listen up! Forget your mothers and everything else you've ever known! You're going up to the line.' Can you imagine saying that—'Forget your mothers!'—to a bunch of terrified kids?" As for his own *madre* (beside her son and proud in the photo at right), Anna is and will always be Tony's life hero. (When I ask if the term applies, he whistles—and no one whistles like Tony Bennett—and drops his eyes, then says, very quietly, "Absolutely.") From *The Good Life,* which is dedicated to her: "My most vivid memory from my childhood is of myself as a 10-year-old boy during the Depression, sitting at my mother's side in our modest home as she worked as a seamstress. Her salary depended on how many dresses she could make and I remember the constant hum of the sewing machine that stopped only long enough for her to cook our dinner." She earns a single penny for each completed dress and yet imparts to Tony a treasured lesson. As he says in conversation: "One of the early gifts I got was from my mother. She always insisted on top quality. She would make those penny dresses, and the more she made, the more she would earn. But even still, she'd throw away a bad dress. Always quality. That's the way to make music that lasts. Like a dress that lasts."

COURTESY OF THE BENEDETTO FAMILY (4)

"I ENJOYED THE MOST MUSICAL freedom I've ever had in my life—I could sing whatever I wanted." So Tony recalled his immediate postwar gig singing swing-era hits like "Blues in the Night" with the Army's Special Services big bands and harmonizing in Army vocal quintets like the one above. While he gains invaluable musical experience, he is also confronted with the kind of open racial prejudice that was widespread throughout the American military during World War II. The experience will make Tony an impassioned and lifelong opponent of bigotry and bigots of every stripe. Thanksgiving, 1945: Tony is stationed in Mannheim, Germany. He has made the rank of corporal in Special Services, and his assignment is, essentially, to do what he loves most: Sing. Strolling through town, Tony is astonished to run into a friend from home. And not just any friend. Frank Smith is a singer and he and Tony used to harmonize together. They were members of the same quartet at the High School of Industrial Arts, back in New York. "I couldn't believe it. Frank Smith in Mannheim, Germany! I was thrilled!" So is Frank, and he takes his old friend to Thanksgiving services at a Baptist church he's miraculously found. Tony in turn invites Frank to join him for a holiday meal at the mess. The two of them get as far as the lobby. An officer in Tony's company approaches in a fury, shouting, "Get your gear, you're pulling out of here!" The superior takes out a razor, cuts Tony's corporal stripes from his shirt, throws them to the ground, spits on them and continues in his rage: "Get your ass out of here!" Tony is demoted and punished—"grave duty; I had to pick up dead bodies," he tells an interviewer decades later. Tony has been caught in blatant defiance of a military rule that is in full force in the aftermath of a war fought to vanquish Hitler's racist Nazi regime. Frank Smith is black, the mess hall is segregated and he is forbidden to break bread with his friend. "No question that incident changed my life forever," Tony tells me. "Frank Smith was just a wonderful guy, and then that ridiculous thing happened—a human nightmare is what it was. To have that happen, in the Army, where you're supposed to be fighting against injustice . . ."

# POP STAR 1947–1964

**"GIRLS GAGA AS TONY CROONS** A HIT." The headline is from the August 26, 1951 Yonkers *Record* and reading it aloud 60 years later is . . . Lady Gaga. In a scene vividly described by author Gay Talese in a 2011 *New Yorker* profile, Tony's son Danny has unearthed the article and he hands it to Gaga as she and Tony get ready to record their vampy version of "The Lady Is a Tramp" for his 2011 *Duets II* album. "See, I told you," Gaga gushes, assuring Tony that she would have been among the bobby-soxers swooning to the sound of his voice when his lush romantic ballad "Because of You" was the smash hit of that long-ago summer. "You make women do that. Look what you did! . . . Oh, Tony, I would have been chasing you around." Gaga, born 35 summers after Tony's debut, will figure prominently in one of his later conquests of pop's pinnacle. Here, in the following pages, is what it is like the first time around.

DON HUNSTEIN/SONY MUSIC ARCHIVES

COURTESY OF THE BENEDETTO FAMILY

"IT WAS AMAZING, EVERYWHERE I went that summer I heard the song blaring from car radios," Tony recalls in *The Good Life* of the first burst of fame that comes with the dizzying success of his debut hit, "Because of You." "My family was thrilled and couldn't stop telling me how proud they were." As his mother, Anna, clearly confirms in the photo at left. The days when she'd come home with her fingers bleeding from seamstress work are behind her for good. With his earnings from his first string of hits—his smash cover of Hank Williams's "Cold, Cold Heart" and "Blue Velvet" among them—he buys Anna a house in River's Edge, New Jersey. For Tony, it's been a long time coming. He'd returned from the Army more determined than ever to make his living as an entertainer. But first, there were dues to be paid, club gigs to be found, day jobs to be endured. And a marquee-worthy name to be had. "I was an elevator operator during the day, but 'Joe Bari' in the clubs—that was my stage name," Tony tells me years later. He would draw attention when he placed second to singer Rosemary Clooney on Arthur Godfrey's popular *Talent Scouts* radio show. "My break came in 1950"—the year the photo opposite was made—"I got a job on Bob Hope's bill at the Paramount, and just before I'm going on, Hope tells me the name's no good. He asks what my real name is. I say Anthony Benedetto. That doesn't do it for him either. So he goes out and says to the audience, 'And here's a new singer, Tony Bennett!' He had to introduce me twice 'cause I didn't know who he was talking about." A year later, everyone knows who Tony Bennett is; at 25 he is the hottest singer in the land. This is the first flowering of Bennettmania, a phenomena that will bloom and fade and bloom again no fewer than three times, in different hues, in decades to come.

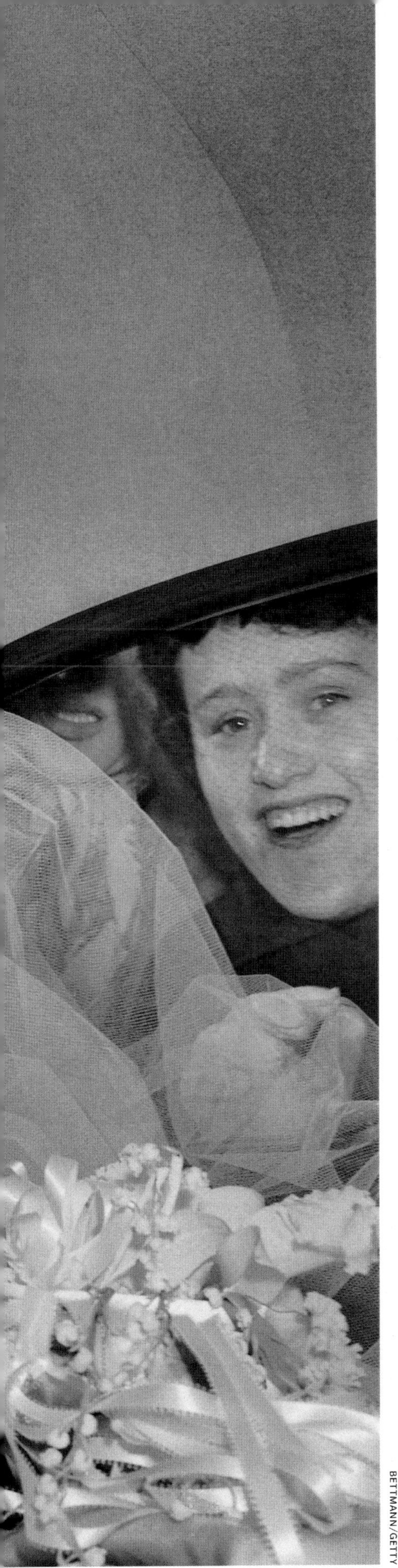

BETTMANN/GETTY

**"GIRLS, DON'T GET TOO EXCITED,** but we have Tony Bennett here." Those are the last words uttered by a Brooklyn girls school headmistress before the surprise guest appears at graduation ceremonies in Brooklyn's Prospect Park. The girls "went wild and started chasing me all over the park," Tony recalls in his memoir. "They tore my clothes, took my cigarettes and everything that I had in my pockets and made me run for my life." Understandably looking for ballast in that mad maelstrom of pop success, Tony finds it in a long distance romance with a fan, Patricia Beech, whom he meets while on tour in Ohio. Soon she moves to New York and the two are wed at St. Patrick's Cathedral on February 12, 1952 (left). When a horde of teenage girls show up in black mourning veils in mock farewell, the press has a field day. But bride and groom are not amused, with Patricia near tears as she struggles to get through the mob and up the stairs of the cathedral. And Tony is furious when he learns the truth: The couple had planed to wed on February 11, but Tony's manager, Ray Muscarella, who has fretted about the effect of marriage on his heartthrob client's career, urges them to push it back a day to February 12, which happens to be Lincoln's Birthday. Muscarella is able to round up hundreds of high school girls on holiday for his publicity stunt; he supplies the veils himself, Patricia never forgives him, and before long Tony replaces Muscarella with a new manager: Tony's sister, Mary—the first but notably not the last time that Tony will trust his career to family.

**TONY FINDS THAT MARRIAGE** hasn't cooled the ardor of his fans. When he and Patricia return from their honeymoon, they find a posse of them camped on the doorstep of their home on Riverside Drive in Manhattan. By the time their first son, D'Andrea, is born in February 1954 (right), the growing family has moved to a spacious four-room apartment overlooking the Hudson in Riverdale, New York. When Tony hears his wife calling the baby Danny, he loves the sound—it reminds him of the pianist Art Tatum playing "Danny Boy" so beautifully at a club on 52nd Street years earlier. At three weeks old Danny, who will grow up to become his father's manager—and help engineer Tony's astonishing return trip to the top of the pops 40 years later—gets an early taste of the life ahead when Tony takes him and Patricia on the road with him. "I was determined," says Tony, "that we stay together."

OSSIE LEVINESS/NY DAILY NEWS ARCHIVE/GETTY

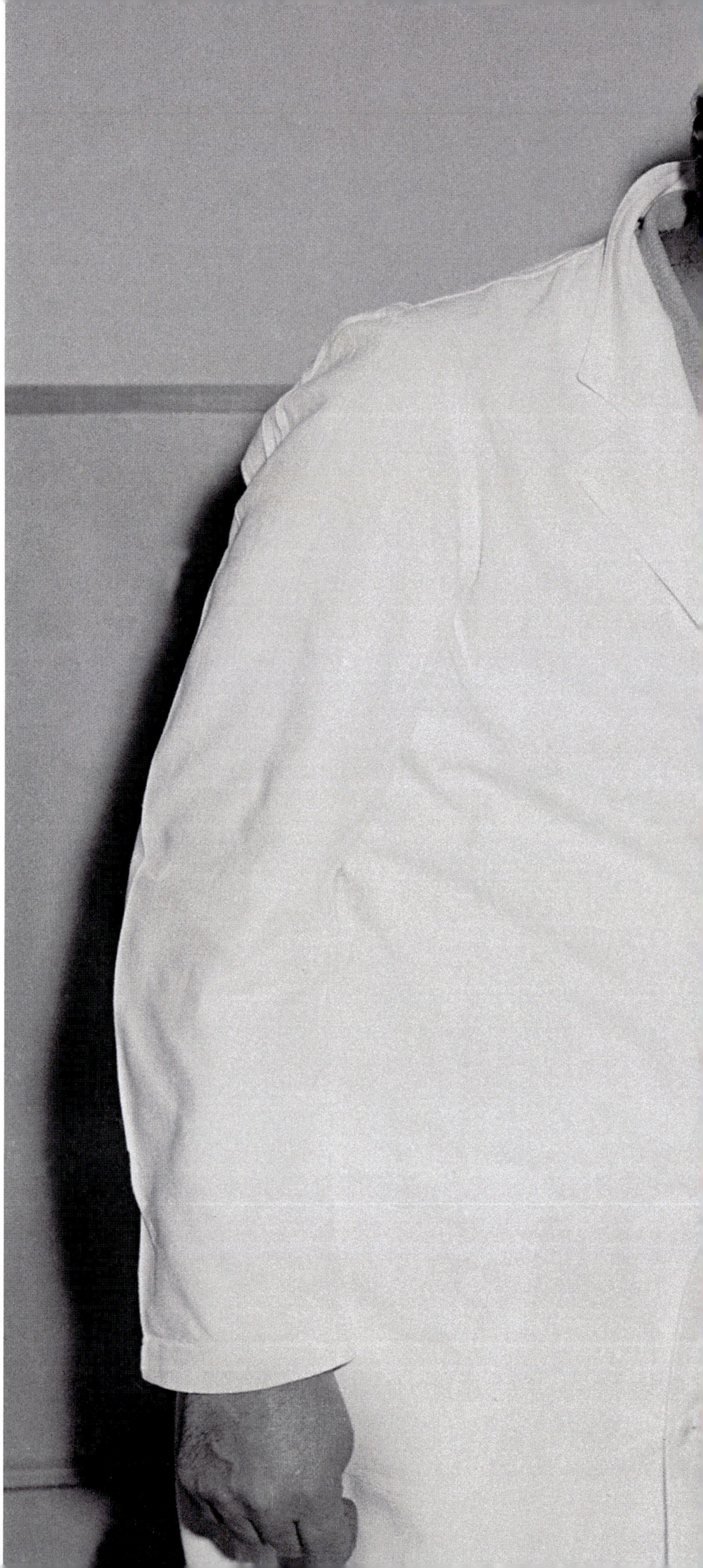

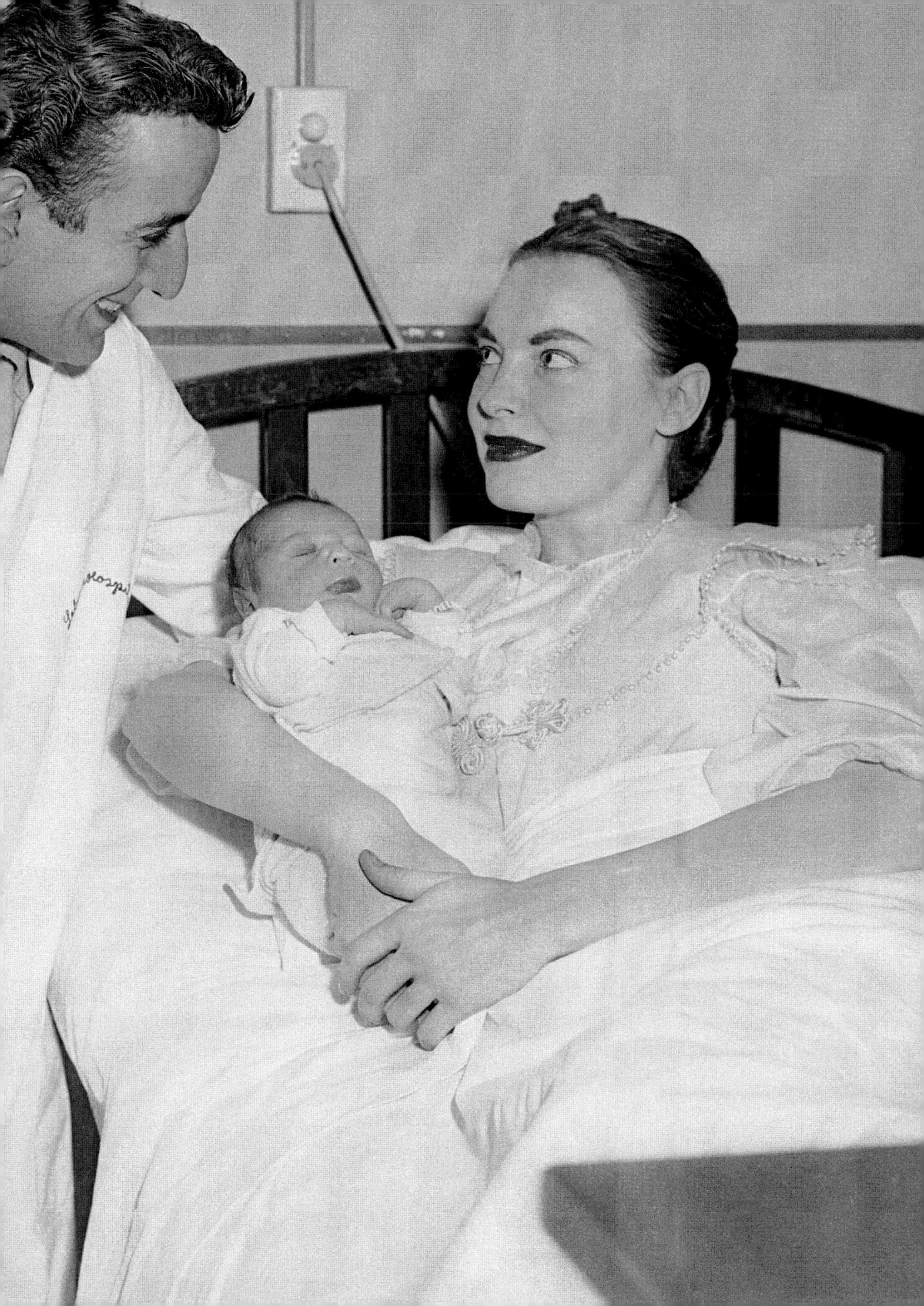

**TONY'S CAREER KEEPS MOVING** in high gear; with extended headlining dates at the Paramount Theater, where as a kid he used to see his hero Frank Sinatra at 75-cent weekday matinees, and at the Copacabana in New York. He and legendary producer Mitch Miller, who becomes a star in his own right with his NBC-TV hit *Sing Along With Mitch,* keep turning out hits like "Rags to Riches" and "Stranger in Paradise." With Tony on the road almost nonstop and away from the family for long stretches, he and Patricia contemplate a move to the suburbs. And so, shortly after their second son, Daegal—it's a Scandinavian name that means "Day"—is born in October 1955, the family moves across the Hudson to New Jersey, eventually settling in Englewood, where they build a house on property once owned by Anne Morrow Lindbergh's family. The photos of Tony and Patricia and their children here and on the following pages are taken two years later, in October 1957. At left, Tony carries Dae and, opposite, Danny plays for his dad. Like his brother, Dae will grow up to play a key role in their father's career, serving as engineer on many of Tony's discs and recording them at his Bennett Sound studios in Englewood. The house that Tony has built there is designed in the Frank Lloyd Wright style, and Tony makes sure to have rooms in the basement designated for music and painting. His big hope for the house is that it might "do Patricia and me some good."

GUY GILLETTE (2)

DAVID MCLANE/NY DAILY NEWS ARCHIVE/GETTY

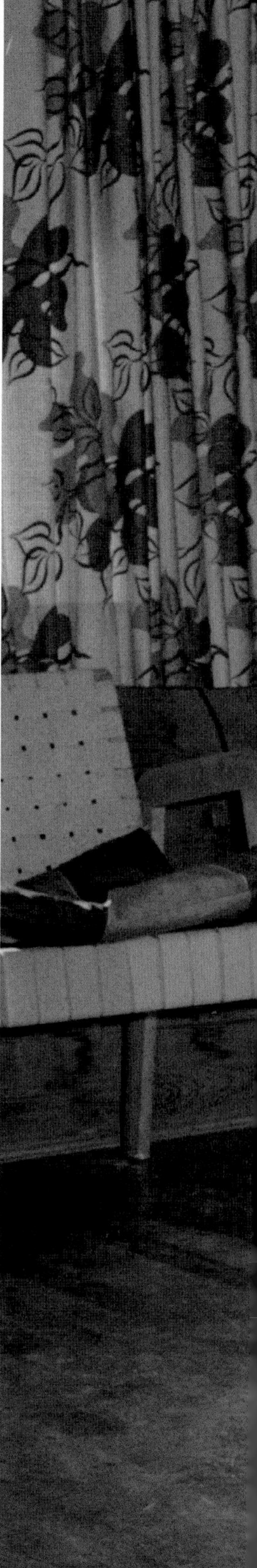

GUY GILLETTE (2)

**PICTURES OF DOMESTIC BLISS** to be sure. But when the photos are shot in 1957, there are already strains in the marriage. After Daegal's birth, it has been decided that Patricia should be home with the boys when Tony tours. The constant separations seriously damage their relationship, and Tony is realizing that you can't fulfill all your dreams just by dreaming them. He wants the solid family life he remembers

from Queens, but he too often is not there to make it happen. Patricia and Tony will separate under the strain and ultimately divorce, though he is determined to remain an important part of his sons' lives—a goal of the heart that will be one of his life's great successes.

DON HUNSTEIN/SONY MUSIC ARCHIVES

IN 1957, AFTER SIX YEARS OF pop stardom achieved as a romantic balladeer, Tony is eager to expand his horizons. He releases what he terms "the most ambitious jazz project of my career. For Tony, *Beat of My Heart* is a labor of love, and one that proves, as a critic writes six decades later, that Tony is much more than a pop star with a "near-operatic" voice—"Here was a man who has jazz chops, musical imagination and a sense of swing." The same year marks the beginning of Tony's long and fruitful musical partnership with pianist Ralph Sharon, whose playing style Tony compares to that of Count Basie. "Ralph Sharon never played a wrong note for me through all those years," Tony says of his accompanist. (Sharon would die in 2015 at age 91). "And his advice [about jazz]! The music I made with Stan Getz, Bill Evans—the jazz giants—those are the best records I ever made in my life."

DON HUNSTEIN/SONY MUSIC ARCHIVES (2)

**THE PICTURES HERE AND ON** the following two pages capture just how exciting Tony Bennett is at the tail end of the '50s—an excitement that he would still stir decades later, in perhaps a less knee-shaking, more debonair style. What isn't conveyed in the photography but is just as important to the audience then and now is Tony's choice of material. He always wants to stick with, as his mother did when making dresses, "quality." The kind he attains in *Beat of My Heart* and again two decades later with *The Art of Excellence*. As we will see in later pages, Tony's determination to perform material built to last rather than bow to current music fashion will become a bone of contention. But here, in these pictures, where he's swinging like nobody's business, he's singing *standards*. And he's making them his own. "I've always gone back to an old piece of advice," Tony says, during a lunch we enjoy at the Metropolitan Museum of Art. "Fred Astaire told me, 'Look at the song through the composer's eyes. Then look at it again with a new idea, but one that's true to what was intended.' See, it's like this." He leans in, and sings lightly as he snaps his fingers. "The way you wear your hat!" It's amazing: His speaking and singing voices are so similar, yet this one floats and flies. The very moment he starts to sing, he becomes the guy on the stage, even as he sits here in an empty dining room. "Or you can think it through again, and do this." He pauses, downshifts. "The way you wear your hat . . ." It's a slow rendering with a backbeat, the last word emphasized—it's the version from his wonderful 1993 Astaire tribute recording, *Steppin' Out*.

"See?" he says. "It breathes differently."

DON HUNSTEIN/SONY MUSIC ARCHIVES (3)

DON HUNSTEIN/SONY MUSIC ARCHIVES

"NO WHITE MAN EVER STOOD in front of a black band and sang with more credentials—and more *belonging*—as did Tony." So says the great Harry Belafonte in the presciently titled documentary *Tony Bennett: The Music Never Ends* directed by Clint Eastwood for PBS in 2007. Belafonte is referring to the years he toured and recorded with the pianist and band leader Count Basie. In this photo, Tony, who is fronting Basie's Orchestra at the Latin Casino in Philadelphia in December 1958, hams it up backstage with trumpeter Joe Newman. "More and more my musical experiences led me to unexpected thrills, like being the first white singer to ever appear on stage with the great Count Basie. Talk about having fun, being with jazz greats like Sonny Payne, Joe Newman, Thad Jones, Snooky Young . . . Those were never-to-be-forgotten days." The collaboration begets two wonderful albums, 1959's *In Person with Count Basie and His Orchestra* and *Count Basie/Tony Bennett: Strike Up the Band* (later rereleased as *Basie Swings, Bennett Sings*). Jazz in this period is morphing just as "pop music" is, but the more avant-garde bebop players, too, appreciate what Tony brings to the table. Said the late trumpet giant Dizzy Gillespie: "Talking about Tony Bennett is the same as a finished musician playing a solo, you don't need 25 choruses to get your message across. I can tell you in a few words. I think Tony's spirituality is so profound in his performance that it cuts through everything superfluous, and what is left is raw soulfulness. Because his philosophy of life is so basic the moment he opens his mouth to sing you know exactly what he is—a prince. I really feel that guy."

**IN JANUARY 1960, TONY IS STILL** fronting the Basie band and clearly, as these pictures testify, having a ball. Around the same time he records songs that will become staples in his performances: "Put On a Happy Face"—"one of the few happy novelty songs I enjoy singing"—"This Time the Dream's on Me" and "The Best Is Yet to Come." About that last record, he says: "In Tin Pan Alley parlance, this is what we call a 'swinger.' I had no idea what would happen with it until one morning, years later, I turned on the radio: The astronauts

SEYMOUR MEDNICK/SONY MUSIC ARCHIVES (2)

who were about to land on the moon were asked how they felt, and they played my recording of 'The Best Is Yet to Come' as an answer. Now, that was . . . far out."

NBCU PHOTO BANK/NBCUNIVERSAL/GETTY

**ON JANUARY 23, 1962, TONY** records "I Left My Heart in San Francisco." It is just what a crooner's career needs as rock 'n' rollers are edging out the prior generation. The same-titled album, released in June, is a hit and the single climbs into the Top 20; it will sell more than 2 million copies, win Tony his first two Grammy awards and become his signature song. In June of '62, the tremendous double disc *Tony Bennett at Carnegie Hall*—still regarded as one of the finest live pop albums of all time—is recorded. Here, at left, on October 1 of the same year, Tony happily drinks in the applause during the very first episode of *The Tonight Show with JoÚny Carson.* Tony tells the story behind the career-shaking song: In the early 1960s, he is still making great music, but is admittedly playing smaller venues—for instance, the Fairmont Hotel in San Francisco. In anticipation of a stint there in 1961, his arranger Ralph Sharon asks George Cory and Douglas Cross, two songwriting partners who had spent time in San Francisco in the '50s, whether they had anything that might strike a Bay Area chord. "Well, we've got this seven-year-old tune called 'I Left My Heart . . .'" Tony, who wears a constant half-smile when it's not a full-blown grin, beams as he talks about that song: "Thank God I like it. I don't think I've ever left it out of a show. I sing it every night."

WESTERN UNION
WESTERN UNION

BOB GOMEL

TONY VISITS WITH PEGGY LEE in her dressing room during a break in her nightclub performance in April 1962. Of the 1950s and early '60s in the business of popular song, he remembers during a casual chat in his apartment on Central Park South: "The competition was intense back then. It was a great era—you had Jo Stafford, Dick Haymes, Nat King Cole, Sarah VaugÚ, Rosemary Clooney, Louis Armstrong, Billy Eckstine, Lena Horne, Judy Garland, Dinah Washington, Peggy Lee, Margaret Whiting. All these great singers. Fierce competition, but there was camaraderie. Sinatra was the one who set the tone." Later I think when Tony reads this, I know what he'll do—he'll slap his forehead and say, "I left out Ella!"

DON HUNSTEIN/SONY MUSIC ARCHIVES

IN SEPTEMBER 1964, TONY IS sporting some truly sporty trousers (left), and circa the same period he is with his mother at a movie premiere (opposite). Which brings us to another interesting period in the career: The Beatles have happened, the boost of "I Left My Heart in San Francisco" and the Carnegie Hall album are now months in the past—months seeming as years—and Tony is, if certainly not at sea, wondering where the future lies. He signs on to play a part in a movie, which will be *The Oscar,* of which the kindest thing said might be: It has a fine theme song ("Maybe September") sung by Tony Bennett. "It's gonna sound a little like I'm name-dropping here," Tony says with a smile, "but I'm not. I hope you realize that. This is about Cary Grant. Some of the best advice I ever got was from Cary Grant. As I said, I had done a little bit in the movies, and I was asking him what I should do in the future. Here he was, this handsome man—the handsomest man in the world. He said to me, 'Don't do films. It's so boring on a set. You love to sing and paint. Follow your passion; those are your passions. Go travel the world and become the best entertainer. You make people feel great—you're alive, they're alive! Sing! Paint!' And it's Cary Grant, right? So I thought I may as well listen."

COURTESY OF THE BENEDETTO FAMILY

# BETWEEN ROCK AND A HARD PLACE 1965–1979

**HE HAS KNOWN THRILLING** highs and terrible lows, but he has never been down like this before. It's Christmas Eve, 1965, and Tony Bennett is spending a long, lonely night by himself at the Gotham Hotel in New York City. His 13-year marriage is on the rocks; his wife and two boys are at the family home in New Jersey, enjoying the holiday as best they can, and he is here, desolate. Careerwise, too, things are less than aces. While he can still get a gig whenever he wants, Tony—who survived the first, Elvis wave of the rock revolution only to get all but swamped by the Beatles and the British invasion—fears his music is slip-sliding out of style. To Tony, at 39, the future looks bleak.

He doesn't have to be here, alone in his room. He could go out, enjoy some wonderful holiday music—his good pal Duke, the grand master whose orchestra has backed Tony on many a memorable occasion, is conducting his Concert of Sacred Music only a few blocks away. But Tony just can't pull himself from the hotel. He climbs into bed and tries to sleep. As he tosses and turns, he hears a strange sound. Figuring he's left the TV on, he gets up but the sound is coming from the hall. Tony opens the door, and there stands the entire chorus from the Sacred Concert caroling "On a Clear Day (You Can See Forever)." Ellington, knowing that his friend is in the dumps, has arranged this private serenade. "Wonderful gesture," Tony recalls at a quiet moment over lunch. "But that night was as bad as it gets."

JOHN DOMINIS/THE LIFE PICTURE COLLECTION/SHUTTERSTOCK (5)

**TO CONTINUE THE STORY—YES** it is a wonderful gesture by the Duke at a point in Tony's life that was as bad as it gets. But something else occurs at roughly the same time that points the way back to the heights, distant as they may be. In a 1965 article in LIFE, Frank Sinatra says: "For my money, Tony Bennett is the best singer in the business. He excites me when I watch him. He moves me. He's the singer who gets across what the composer has in mind, and probably a little more." As Tony tells me years later: "That quote would

change my life. Frank was always such a generous man." The impact of Sinatra's encomium? "Since then," Tony tells interviewers, "I sold out around the world." Opposite are four outtakes from JoÚ Dominis's 10,000-image epic on Sinatra at age 50, shot for LIFE; above Frank and Tony chow down on frankfurters after Frank's show in Miami.

"DUKE ELLINGTON AND I WERE close friends," Tony tells the *Wall Street Journal* decades later. How close? "So close that his entire band once came over to my mother's house in New Jersey for an Italian dinner." Here, circa 1965, the Duke is cutting a cake nearly big enough to provide dessert for the whole gang; and (opposite) he's with Tony at the eighth annual Grammys, at which he wins honors for his *Ellington '66* LP. Tony is a fellow with a long memory and he will never forget or forgive incidents 10 years apart when first Duke and later his friend Nat King Cole are refused service in the very Miami hotels where they are star

MICHAEL OCHS ARCHIVES/GETTY

NBCU PHOTO BANK/NBCUNIVERSAL/GETTY

attractions. "Nat and Duke were geniuses, brilliant human beings who gave the world some of the most beautiful music it's ever heard," Tony writes in his memoir, "and yet they were treated like second-class citizens. The whole situation enraged me." And so: "When Harry Belafonte called and asked me to join Martin Luther King's civil rights march in Selma, Alabama, in 1965, I accepted."

CHARLES MOORE/GETTY IMAGES

**HERE ARE HARRY BELAFONTE** and Tony, flanking the Reverend Martin Luther King Jr. in Selma, Alabama, in the spring of 1965. Harry is an old friend of Tony's from the days when both were struggling musicians hanging out at Hanson's Drug Store on Manhattan's Swing Street and hoping for a gig at any of the live music clubs that lined that magical block of 52nd Street. Now Harry has recruited Tony to join a roster of celebrities including Tony's friend Billy Eckstine, Leonard Bernstein, Sammy Davis Jr. and other music and film stars to march alongside King through the heart of the Jim Crow South, from Selma to Montgomery. Invited to draw media attention to King's voting rights campaign, the notables will need more courage than is required of today's most activist stars. "I remember on the march, I noticed Jilly Rizzo, Sinatra's right-hand man, marching right next to me," Tony recalls during a lunch at an Italian eatery on the East Side. "I looked at him and I see he's got these brass knuckles on. He's wearing them! And he looks at me and says, 'Just in case any of these guys want trouble.' And I say, 'Jilly, this is supposed to be a peace march!'" Despite Tony's humor in recounting the incident, it was hardly fun and games on the march. The threat of violence was constant, the mood ever ominous. Tony will long remember the open hostility of police and the jeering on-lookers all along the march route and how, he writes, "we tried to act cool and pretend we weren't terrified by the violence that surrounded us." Later, he is sickened and horrified when he finds out that Viola Liuzzo, a white volunteer from Detroit—the same woman who drives Tony and Billy Eckstine to the airport to catch their flights home—has been murdered by Klansmen after dropping other marchers at the airport.

IT SURE LOOKED LIKE THE perfect launch vehicle for stage two of Tony's career. But as discussed earlier, despite the can't miss title, 1965's *The Oscar* was a bust and Tony's Hollywood movie career was grounded at take off. Though he would get offers for other film roles, "my heart just wasn't in it," he writes in *The Good Life*. "Acting didn't hold the charm for me that performing, making records and painting does." But it is while filming *The Oscar* that Tony meets the woman who will become his second wife, 25-year-old beauty Sandra Grant. Herself an aspiring actress (and former paramour of baseball great Joe DiMaggio) she and Tony, pictured together in the photo at right in London in 1968, begin their romance as his marriage to Patricia is dissolving. By 1970, his long relationship with Columbia Records is likewise on the skids. Tony has been drained by constant battles with the label's new president, Clive Davis, over Davis's insistence that his traditional pop artists cover contemporary chart-toppers. "Those were such stupid days," says Tony's son Danny, himself a rock musician before he became his father's manager. "They were telling Streisand to sing Dylan songs. So stupid." Not surprisingly then, 1970's *Tony Sings the Great Hits of Today!* proves a last straw and the singer, whose hits of yesterday helped turn Columbia into a music industry powerhouse, finally walks. "I just couldn't stand it," he says one afternoon at his apartment, the sun shining in through the windows. "I actually regurgitated when I made that awful album—I got physically sick. You see, if I really adore a song, I just get into that creative zone and try to get the definitive version of the song that would make the composer feel magnificent. Where he would say, 'That's what I was trying to convey.' And Columbia wasn't letting me do that anymore." So he leaves the label, with one exec warning that Tony will never be heard from again. In 1971, as Tony sets out to prove the suit wrong, he and Sandra are wed and soon Tony enters into what he calls "my English period." Harkening to advice he'd once been given by the bandleader Ted Lewis—"Do yourself a favor. Play England every year. The fans are unlike anywhere else in the world. They're loyal. They never forget you"—he relocates to London, where Lewis is proved right. In 1972, Tony, now with a new young family—he and Sandra welcome daughters Joanna and Antonia during their relationship—sells out concerts all over Great Britain, stars in a variety TV series and records albums for a new label, MGM/ Verve. "I worked hard while I was in England," Tony writes in his memoir, "but I also took some time for my personal life, something I hadn't done in years." And, he adds, "I'd been painting whenever I could but it was in London that I really started to get serious about it." He also took up tennis, another passion that would remain with him the rest of his life.

BOB DEAR/AP

DON HUNSTEIN/SONY MUSIC ARCHIVES

**FOR TONY, IT HAS ALWAYS** been a family affair. "I got my first encouragement as a child from my family when they would sit in a circle on Sunday afternoons and ask my brother, sister and I to perform for them. It was during those days that I discovered that I wanted to be an entertainer," Tony will recall late in life. "So to have my own family participating with me now is a blessing." And here we have the future power trio: Tony with his sons Dae (left), who will serve as his father's producer (and win himself a Grammy for the 2016 tribute album *Tony Bennett Celebrates 90*), and Danny, who as Tony's manager will help turn his career around and make good himself, rising to become the head of a major record label. Though the boys' mother, Patricia, and Tony separate in the mid-'60s and divorce in 1971, Tony takes great care to stay close with his sons, as they readily acknowledge—some of their memories being nothing short of magical. "Prior to my folks' split, I remember a wonderful childhood," Danny tells *Good Housekeeping* magazine in 1995. "I remember waking up to hear Count Basie and Duke Ellington jamming in our basement. Even after the divorce, I remember my father as always being around. I was proud of him. Not many know that before it became fashionable among celebrities, my dad marched for civil rights in Selma, Alabama, and refused to play South Africa because of apartheid. He is a good man and a good father." And his sons never doubt his destiny, despite predictions that he was finished after he left Columbia. "No way he could've stopped then," says Danny. "It's not about making money, it's about making music. I'm his son, but about one thing I can be objective—he is one of those people who has to do what they do. He will die singing."

EVENING NEWS/SHUTTERSTOCK

"SANDRA, JOANNA AND I TOOK in the lovely English sights and got to spend some good times together," recalls Tony of a happy period spent abroad. Here is the family, newly arrived in rainy London, on January 3, 1972. In the photo opposite, they're at the London Zoo in Regent's Park later that month. In two years they will become a family of four. But brewing troubles would soon make it hard to imagine the marvels the following decades have in store.

CSU ARCHIVES/EVERETT/ALAMY

TOM VANO

HERE TONY IS AT WORK WITH jazz genius Bill Evans on the first of two brilliant piano-and-voice collaborations they would produce in the 1970s—both treasured recordings today. While Tony lauds Evans as "the greatest and most influential jazz pianist of his generation," Evans—whose place in the pantheon of hip was enshrined on Miles Davis's seminal 1959 LP *Kind of Blue*—is a devoted Tony Bennett fan, as he makes clear in a radio interview broadcast when the two opened the Newport Jazz Festival at Carnegie Hall in 1976: "Occasionally fans act surprised by the fact that Tony and I have joined together because they tend to see Tony in the superstar pop singer image. But you know, every great jazz musician I know idolizes Tony—from Philly Joe Jones to Miles Davis, you name it. The reason is that Tony is a great musical artist. He puts music first, and it's just a joy to work with somebody like that." Their recordings—*The Tony Bennett/Bill Evans Album,* released in 1975, and its follow up, 1977's *Together Again*—are magical summit meetings, and the music is sublime. Sadly, Evans, long in the grip of addictions, will suffer a tragically early death in 1980 at age 51. Shortly before his death, Evans tracks Tony down in a small Texas town where he is staying while on the road. "Bill, what are you calling me here for?" Tony asks. In a desperate tone, Evans says, "I wanted to tell you one thing: Just think truth and beauty. Forget about everything else. Just concentrate on truth and beauty, that's all." The phrase becomes something of a mantra for Tony, even after it takes on a shadow of tragedy with Evans's death. That event, says Tony, "made me think hard about my own drug use." It would take a few more years for Tony to clean up his own bad habits, but the thinking had begun: *I want to survive. I want to be around.*

RICHARD CORKERY/NY DAILY NEWS ARCHIVES/GETTY (2)

TONY AND SANDRA'S SECOND daughter, Antonia, is born in the spring of 1974. (A professional singer today, she tours regularly with her dad throughout his final decades.) Not long after Antonia's arrival, the family departs for new horizons. "I now had two beautiful daughters and we moved to Los Angeles and started living the glamorous Hollywood lifestyle—the good and the bad," Tony will recall in his memoir. Rocky times are ahead, but as these photos from 1977 attest, family life brings joy. Opposite: Six-year-old Joanna. Above: Antonia has the sniffles.

RICHARD CORKERY/NY DAILY NEWS ARCHIVES/GETTY

**HERE ARE TONY AND JOANNA** in June 1977, about midway through the family's sojourn in La-La Land, where, as Tony recalls in *The Good Life*, things aren't *all* bad: "We had the big beautiful house in Beverly Hills, the celebrity friends, and the endless round of parties." The highlights, hands down, are the deep friendships with Fred Astaire, Ella Fitzgerald, Frank Sinatra, and others. JoÚny Carson, both a fan and a friend since Tony's featured appearance on that first *Tonight Show* broadcast back in '62, invites him to perform—and to bring along new paintings to show the folks. Thus is Tony introduced to his fans as a visual artist. It's possible that Carson has heard about Tony's talent from the first person to whom the artist makes a sale—their mutual friend Cary Grant. But before long Tony finds himself seduced by a new form of Hollywood stardust. "Cocaine flowed as freely as champagne," he confesses in his memoir, "and soon I began joining in the festivities." Pot smoking didn't help, and suddenly "the whole thing started sneaking up on me." At the same time, his marriage is destabilizing and the record label he cofounded in 1975, Improv, isn't working out as well financially as it has musically. "One thing I'm not is a businessman," he writes. Recounting a vivid moment of truth, Tony tells *Good Housekeeping* magazine of an evening when, after a postconcert party in Las Vegas, he looks down from the balcony of his hotel and sees a lonely man walking the streets: "It was like a light bulb went off in my head. Very quickly I came to realize all I needed to make me happy was a drumroll, a band and some people who want me to sing. Looking back, I know I grew up only when I was already in my forties."

# "I WANNA BE AROUND" 1980–1990

**"I WENT THROUGH IT ALL, I** had entourages, party after party. I walked away and said, 'What a waste of time.' Everyone expected something great to happen and it never did," says Tony, succinctly dissecting the previous decade's empty excesses—like a New Year's Eve party that never lives up to its giddiest expectation—in a conversation with *Entertainment Weekly*'s Betty Goodwin. His hangover cure? "It was a search for the right way to do things." He finds it at the dawn of the '80s, after experiencing losses in his bank account and marriage alike. He wouldn't make it without his sons' help. This is the birth of the solid family team that will nurture Tony's remarkable twilight renaissance—one of the greatest, most sustained late-season rises in the history of American entertainment. Tony shakes his drug habit and Danny straightens out his finances and prepares to introduce Tony to a new and hip young audience. His relationship with Sandra—and L.A.—has waned and when she serves him divorce papers, Tony returns to New York, alone. Sad news, and yet: Gears have shifted. Tony is going forth into a new tomorrow.

PHOTOGRAPH © HARRY BENSON

**THE ART OF EXCELLENCE: NO TITLE** could better express Tony's musical creed and holy grail—his demand for quality—and here he is performing a duet with its very embodiment, the genius of soul, Ray Charles. The two are in Larrabee Studios in Los Angeles on January 4, 1986, recording James Taylor's "Everybody Has the Blues," one of *Excellence*'s dozen tracks.

Tony resists calling it a comeback—"I was always working," he says and his 200 shows a year tour schedule so attests—but the album is his first in nearly a decade and it heralds not only his return to Columbia after a 14-year absence, but a turnaround, for his career and in his life. "I Wanna Be Around," he sang in the '60s and he will be, for decades to come, but he never dreamed it would happen like this, finding a brand-new audience for the Great American Songbook classics that have always been his staple. "I asked Count Basie if I should try rock," Tony says to me one day. "Basie told me in that sly, wise way of his. 'Why change an apple?'" And of course Tony never will again. Instead of pandering to the MTV set, he charms them, making regular appearances on David Letterman and MTV itself and even *The Simpsons*—asked to contribute to the soundtrack, he becomes a recurring animated character. Tony claims he isn't surprised by his appeal to the grandchildren of his first fans because, he writes, "I was positive they would embrace the music I'd sung all my life." At the same time, he is thankful that he is still around, afterall, to enjoy it. As he says in an interview with the *Boston Globe*: "I used to take pills. Uppies. Downies. Sleepies. But no more. I'm in touch with myself. I'm healthier now than I have ever been. And I've become unbuggable." *Unbuggable*. What a fine Tony Bennett word.

BARBARA CROWNOVER/AP

**THE ARTIST AT WORK, AS SEEN** in this photograph by Harry Benson, a great friend of LIFE's since the 1960s, is a man in tune—with himself, with his art, with his surroundings. When Benson visits his studio, a few floors down from his apartment in midtown Manhattan in 1986—the same year as it happens that *The Art of Excellence* sets his recording career back on the upswing—he is at work on a portrait of Judy Garland, a friend dear to him and lost. "When I look back," he writes in his memoir, recalling the last time he saw her—ribbing him after a performance two months before she died in 1969—"it's hard to believe that most of the time she was just trying to hold on for dear life." For Tony, painting and sketching are lifelong passions, as important to him as music. He can't imagine life with one and not the other; it's always been like that for him. When he was little and all the relatives would fill the family apartment in Astoria on Sunday afternoons, "I would sing for them and also show them my art," he recalls in a London *Daily Mail* interview. "I remember clearly saying this is who I am." By the age of 12 he is already an untrained master of doodles, classroom caricatures and elaborate color chalk sidewalk murals, when he is taken under wing by his junior high art teacher, who becomes a lifelong friend. He learns from him, Tony writes, "how important it is to be honest with yourself in order to do good work—to be as objective as possible [and] willing to do the work needed to make it better."

In high school—he attends New York's Industrial Arts—he is intent on studying art, learning to work in oils and watercolors and picking up skills from silk-screening to stained glass window making. And all the while, he's singing every chance he gets, applying wisdom he learns from music in his painting and vice versa. From the drummer Louie Bellson he learns the secret of free form—"'You can't successfully break the rules until you learn what rules you're breaking,'" Tony recalls in his memoir. And from painstaking struggles to orchestrate harmonies with color and light at the easel, he learns "never to give up, keep going, keep plowing through." The next take just may be the keeper. Always more than a dabbler—he will still

PHOTOGRAPH © HARRY BENSON

be taking lessons into his eighties—Tony turns pro with that first sale, to no less a client than Cary Grant. "It was a scene in the south of France," Tony tells an interviewer. "He liked it because the view from his window in the Hollywood Hills looked very similar to the painting." By next millenium, Bennett, who signs his art work with his given name, Anthony Benedetto, will have paintings hanging in the Smithsonian, and his work will command high five-figure prices. Always, when on the road, he packs sketch pad and paints along with his tuxedos."Painting is a vacation for me at all times," he tells me on a visit to his studio. "As I travel, I'm on vacation, sketching and singing. These are the things I love to do." He adds, quoting Michelangelo, "that is the whole premise of what I do—the search. I'm looking to grow, to learn."

E.J. CAMP

"THE MORE RELAXED A THING is, the more peaceful it is," Tony, the very picture of what he speaks in the photo at left (from 1992), tells *EW's* Betty Goodwin. "It's almost like water on a rock. The water's so simple, so powerful, it molds the rock." Spoken like a Zen master. And what wonders peacefulness and contentment—brought in part by his interest in Eastern mysticicsm, but moreso, perhaps, by the new love in his life, future bride Susan Crow—have wrought. As Ralph Sharon, Tony's longtime accompaniest, tells Goodwin, the days of turmoil and strife are long gone. "There's a simpleness to Tony's life." As if to prove the point, Tony, after a light dinner and a white wine spritzer, Goodwin notes, "excuses himself to practice his scales."

# "THE BEST IN THE BUSINESS" 1991–2023

**"THE MAN'S AMAZING. TRULY** great! His rhythm, his style, the way he grabs a tune . . ." The speaker is Elvis Costello, the onetime angry young man who spearheaded rock's New Wave in the 1980s. It is late 1994 and Elvis has been watching in the wings as 58-year-old Tony Bennett, silver haired and dapper, winds up a two-and-a-half-hour set of standards—the same stuff he was singing in '65 and in '55, '75 and '85 too—before a packed house in New York City. At this moment he is one of the hottest acts in the business. His concerts are sellouts, and his last two albums—*Perfectly Frank* and *Steppin' Out*—his tributes to musical heroes Frank Sinatra and Fred Astaire—have scored Grammys two years running. The soundtrack of tonight's *MTV Unplugged* set will be the biggest seller of his career. This evening he closes his performance with a rendition of a chestnut, "Fly Me to the Moon." As cheers rain down, he clasps his hands (as he does in a 1998 Radio City concert, right) in a gesture that expresses how genuinely moved he is. He is also thankful and not a little incredulous that 44 years into his career, he is the darling of the MTV generation. "And all I'm doing," he says, "is what I've always done—sing good songs."

CHRIS OTTAUNICK/SONY MUSIC ARCHIVES

JASON KEMPIN/GETTY

**LOVE IS HERE TO STAY AND SO** is Tony, 92 in 2018 when he and jazz siren Diana Krall (in Nashville, above) score a hit album of Gershwin tunes. It caps the third installment of Tony's career as a time-transcending American idol: After setting the bobby sox and saddle shoes set to swooning in the '50s and wowing slackers in the '90s, Tony helps legions of new millenium fans discover the wonders of the Great American Songbook with his 2007 Grammy-winning best-seller, *Duets: An American Classic* and its 2011 follow-up, *Duets II*. The albums team him with such diverse masters of song as Aretha Franklin, Willie Nelson, and two 21st-century pop heroines, one tragic, Amy Winehouse, and one triumphant, Lady Gaga. His later outing with Gaga yields *Cheek to Cheek*, another blast from pop's elegant past that debuts at No. 1 on *Billboard*'s Top 200 album chart, making Tony, then a dewy 88, the oldest to accomplish the feat since, well, Tony Bennett did it with *Duets II*. (Opposite: With Gaga in Vegas, top, and Billy Joel in New York, in 2019.

KEVIN MAZUR/PARK MGM LAS VEGAS/GETTY

KEVIN MAZUR/EXPLORING THE ARTS/GETTY

E.J. CAMP (2)

**ROOMS WITH A VIEW: AS IS CLEAR** from the photo above, Tony likes to paint scenes that he sees from his window. And because he is on the road as many as 200 days a year when these pictures are taken in his midtown Manhattan studio, he has amassed a goodly collection of city scapes, roof tops and street scenes framed by hotel and dressing room windows he's gazed from the world over. But soon, he will come to favor a singular view above all others. Seated in the Trustees Dining Room at the Metropolitan Museum of Art on a gray winter afternoon, Tony is gazing out the enormous windows overlooking Central Park. "I love that park," he says softly. "I always dreamed of having a place that would catch the afternoon light, so I could paint the park over and over." His fond wish has long since come true. Shortly after our lunch, Tony and his then-future wife Susan—"She's wonderful," he says when she's gone to make a phone call, "I really love her so much"—move into the sprawling apartment on Central Park South that will be their home ever after. With spectacular views of the park and a studio with skylights that catch that afternoon light by the bucketful, Tony, who will reduce his road work to a couple of dozen shows a year, could lay claim to true happiness: "All it takes," he says, "is a standard song to sing and an easel on which to paint."

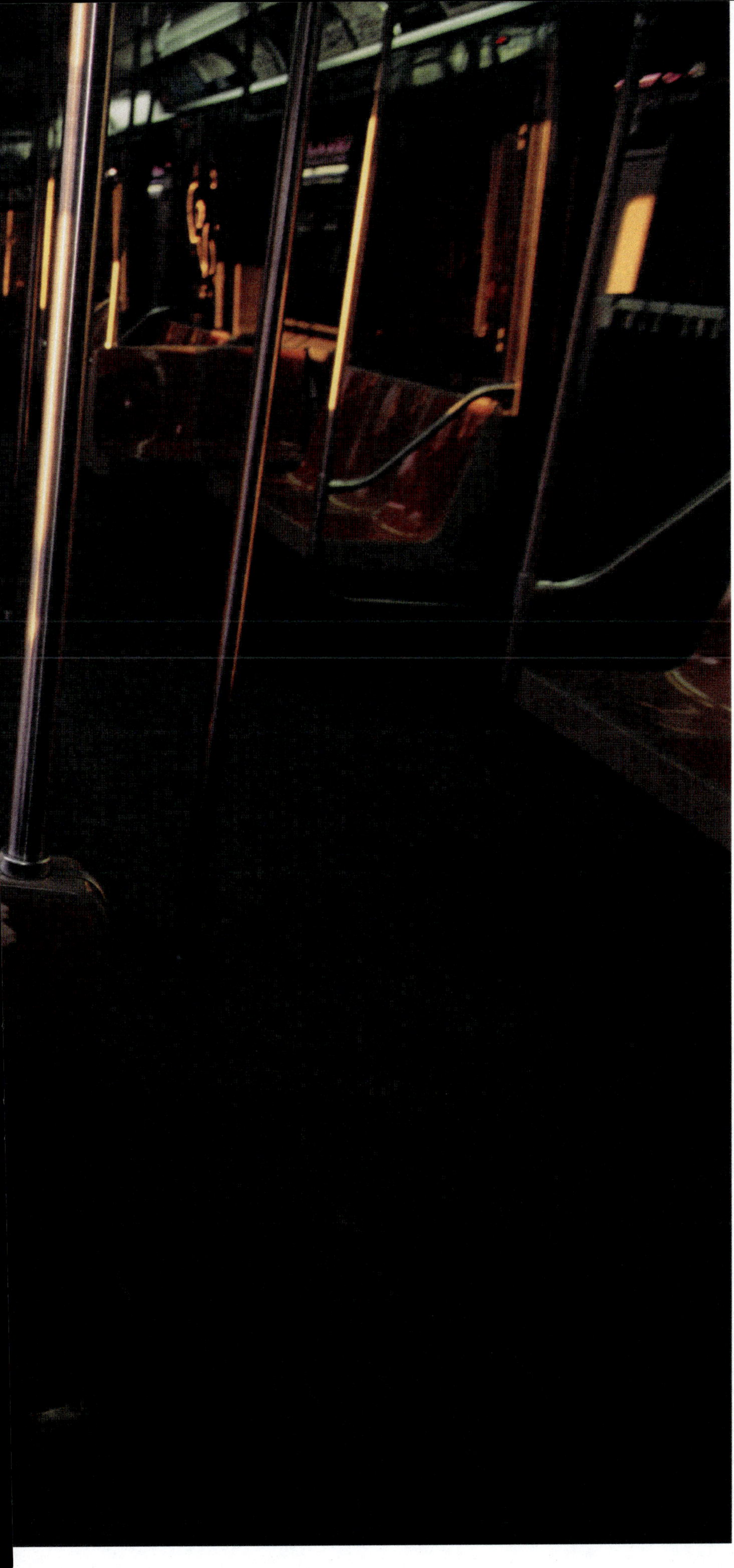

JOE MCNALLY/CONTOUR/GETTY

**THOUGH HE'S ALWAYS BEEN** a news junkie, ripped-from-the-headlines has never been Tony's style. Affairs of the heart, not issues of the day, are the stuff of lasting popular song. As he recalls from the days of his first big break in the late 1940s when Bob Hope gives him a new name and a fantastic gig, as a member of his variety show troupe at the Paramount Theater in Times Square: "I remember doing a narration about how it was great being home from the war with all your army buddies, and I started getting booed," Tony tells music writer John Lewis in 2009. "They just wanted to hear love songs. See, everybody was tired of the war. So I took it out of the show." Here (and on several more of the pages in this part of our book) is one of the wonderful portraits made by Joe McNally for the 1995 LIFE feature on Tony. At left he is indulging his daily newspaper habit on the New York subway—growing up it was his lifeline from his home in Queens to Manhattan, his city of dreams.

© JOE MCNALLY

**"I'VE BEEN ALL OVER THE** world—Paris and Florence and Capri—and yet I come back here and I like this better than any place I've ever lived." It is 2009, and Tony is telling a *New York Times* reporter about the marvels, not of storied Manhattan, but the unglamorous borough of Queens. His love for the place is rooted in his past but it also holds a piece of his future and legacy. The Frank Sinatra School of the Arts opens its doors in 2001, with Sinatra having nothing to do with it beyond inspiration. Tony and his wife, Susan—after more than 20 years together the couple wed in 2007—raise the funds and shepherd the school into existence, with New York City including it in its massive public schools system. In 2009 the school moves from its original home in neighboring Long Island City into a new and airy, architecturaly splendid five-story building in Astoria. The school offers theater, dance, film, fine arts and of course music programs. Among the school's state-of-the-art facilities, which include film production and recording studios, is the Tony Bennett Concert Hall. Friends of Tony's who visit the school to talk with students, offer instruction and entertain over the years include Jerry Seinfeld, Wynton Marsalis, Bruce Willis and Paul McCartney. In 2014, Lady Gaga—*A Star is Born* since proving Tony's long voiced predictions that film fame awaits her—performs at the school shortly after McCartney does the same. "Paul McCartney is one of my idols," says then-sophomore Melina McGaw, a visual arts student. "I sat three seats away from Tony Bennett that day. We always have one surprise guest each year, but this year, after Paul McCartney, we also had Lady Gaga. Everyone got really excited. Seeing her sing this old, beautiful music—she's so talented, it was just great."

**PHOTOGRAPHER JOE MCNALLY'S** shot of Tony as he gazes from a Queens diner catches him in a reflective mood. Even as he enjoys his resurgent career, it is a time for poignant looking back, as he does a few years later when his friend and mentor Frank Sinatra passes away in 1998. "I was one of the original Sinatra groupies," Tony writes in a rememberance published under his byline in *Entertainment Weekly.* "Back when I was [in high school] I would get out of classes to see Tommy Dorsey's orchestra at the Paramount. I'd stay for seven shows a day and watch Sinatra over and over again." A star himself by 1956, Tony suffered a crippling bout of stage fright. "I was so desperate I decided to go see Frank for advice, even though we had never met. When I told people, 'I'm going to go see Sinatra!' everybody said 'Stay away! He's tough! Look out!.'" But I knocked on his dressing room door and he opened it and said, 'Come in, Tony.' I was surprised he even knew me! I told him how nervous I was [on stage] and he said not to worry about that. 'Audiences don't mind when you're nervous. They'll see that you really want to get over and they'll support you.' Frank not only gave me confidence; he gave me a great lesson. Being excited is an essential part of performing; those butterflies mean you care. Through the years the wonderful things Frank said about me really helped build my audience. One of the first compliments Frank paid me has always stayed with me: 'Tony, you can only be yourself — but you're very good at that.' No matter how you express yourself, it comes out of yourself. It comes from your head and your heart. I asked him years later, 'Why do you think you and I have stayed around so long?' He said, 'There's no mystery; it's because we stayed with good songs.' And he was right."

LUNCH
GATE CORP.
(212) 657-3713
WE
729
GYROS
GYROS
GYROS
PIZZA ON
Phone

ON A TOUR OF THE OLD neighborhood in 1995, Tony reminisces with his son Danny on the stoop of the building in Astoria where he grew up during the Depression. Despite his family's struggles to make ends meet following the early death of his father, Tony remembers a happy childhood. "It's funny," he tells writer John Lewis in 2009, "in the middle of deep poverty, it was the warmest time of my life." Boyhood in Astoria was like something out of the Dead End Kids movies, says Tony, who ran with a gang of mischief-making kids, raised pigeons on the roof and revelled in the neighborhood's ethnic mix. "It was a perfect place to grow up," he writes in his memoir. "Instead of being surrounded only by Italian Americans, [there] were Irish, Polish, Greek, Italian and Jewish families living side by side. I remember the Irish families were especially fond of the Mills Brothers, and Irish quartets hung out on street corners and sang traditional rhythm and blues songs like 'Paper Doll.' It was kind of surreal." Flash forward to another happily bewildering moment in Tony's life, this one of Danny's making. It is 1994 and four decades after a pack of screaming teenage school girls were chasing him across Prospect Park, Tony is beseiged once again, this time by Gen X kids young enough to be his grandchildren. "It was like you were the Beatles," Susan says of the young American fans who swarmed him on a recent trip to Italy. "It's been crazy, this whole thing with the kids," admits Tony. "My son Danny did all that. He'd been managing me for a while and he said "Just trust me, Dad.' He got me on *The Simpsons,* then MTV. I said, 'Hey's what's going on? I'm used to playing nice rooms.' He said, 'Trust me.' And all of a sudden—kids!"

2314

© JOE MCNALLY

**WHERE BETTER TO BID** farewell than in the city by the bay—and in the arms of the woman who gives Tony's signature song of heartbreak a happy ending. A quarter century after he sang about leaving his heart in San Francisco, he finds it in that very city when, in the late 1980s, he falls in love with Susan Crow Benedetto, a Bay Area native and onetime president of the local Tony Bennett fan club. After a nearly 20-year courtship, they wed in 2007 and friends say Tony has never been in a more stable relationship, or happier. Their love, he says in *Just Getting Started*, a 2016 memoir, has given him the courage to be his "best self." And as Sinatra advised him long before, therein lies the secret of success, in art as in life. "He said to keep three things in mind" when performing, daughter Antonia tells *AARP Magazine* in 2009, recalling professional advice imparted by her father: "Breathe before each phrase; sing as if you're telling a story; and if you sing the word 'love' make sure you mean it." As record producer Phil Ramone put it, neatly summing up both Tony Bennett's legacy and his pan-generational appeal: "He sings from the heart, and you want to be in the company of his voice, no matter what age you are." So it seems in April 2018, as Tony, age 91, winds up an 80-minute concert at the Winspear Opera House in Dallas. First comes what a reviewer calls the "aching nostalgia" of "I Left My Heart in San Francisco," and then a spellbinding rendition of "Fly Me to the Moon." As Tony sets aside his microphone and steps to the front of the stage, the theater rings with the sound of his voice, "unamplified," notes the reviewer, and "bursting with life."

# WHY I SING

KELSEY BENNETT

*"We're put here to sing—this family was put here to sing. I've always felt that right through my life, right up to today as I speak to you. I just feel that I have to do it . . . The Benedettos had to sing."*

Here, in 2011, in a photograph taken by his granddaughter Kelsey, Tony sings "'O Sole Mio" on the mountaintop in Calabria.